Edith Münzer

GRAZ

121 Photographs in colour

BONECHI VERLAG STYRIA

Vertrieb
für Österreich
VERLAG STYRIA
Schönaugasse 64
A-8010 GRAZ

für Deutschland
Butzon & Bercker GmbH
Hooge Weg 71
D-47623 Kevelaer

für die Schweiz
Herder AG Basel
Muttenzerstraße 109
CH-4133 Pratteln 1

© Copyright by
CASA EDITRICE BONECHI, Via Cairoli 18/b
I-50131 Florence

E-mail: bonechi@bonechi.it
Internet: www.bonechi.it

Printed in Italy by the Centro Stampa Editoriale Bonechi.

Photographs from the Archives of Casa Editrice Bonechi taken by Luigi di Giovine

ISBN 3-222-11413-7

◀ *A view of the city in the Chapel of the Treasury of the Mariahilfe Convent.*

A GLANCE BACKWARDS

Graz is an old city and, as with many other cities, this works entirely to its advantage (as long as she knows to take care of her venerable aspect, which is precisely the case with Graz). The provincial capital of Styria celebrated her 850th anniversary, to be exact, in 1978. In point of fact, the city was mentioned for the first time in the year 1128 in a rather controversial document.

Various hypotheses exist concerning the origin of her name, but only one is valid enough. From the time they are school children, the inhabitants of Graz learn the legend which tells of the origin of the city's name. When Bavarian colonists, who had been called into the country by the Slavonians to help them fend off the Avars, were asked how the construction of the city was coming along, they answered, "G'räts, so g'räts" ("Alright, alright"). From this expression came the term "Graz", which still in the last century, however, was called "Grätz". At that time, there was heated discussion among the distinguished citizens of the town about how the name of the city should finally be written: "Graz" or "Grätz".

In truth, however, "Graz" derives from the Slavic "gradec", which means "little castle", (probably the fortification on the Schlossberg was a Slavic stronghold at one time).

Right from the start, the enemy came from the Orient. It is from there that the Avars came, a people of nomadic horsemen, bringers of death and destruction. Emperor Charlemagne annihilated them toward the end of the VIIIth century. In the IXth century, though, a new and dangerous enemy loomed up, the Magyars who ceased their incursions only after their decisive defeat at Lechfeld in 955.

Emperor Otho the Great created the Karantania March to defend the Duchy of the same name which the city of Graz was once a part of, but the most important locality of this March was not yet Graz, but rather Hengistburg near Wildon, a legendary fortress no longer extant which, for a long time, was thought to be located in Graz.

In the XIth century, the Traungaus, a family of Baverian counts, arrived in the Karantania March. From their main castle, Steyr, they took on the name of Margraves of Steyr. This is how the name of Steiermark (Styria) was born. Steyr today, in any case, no longer belongs to the Green March, but instead to Upper Austria. The Karantania March succeeded from Carinthia, thus becoming Styria.

The minute and fortified town, which was Graz, grew thanks to the immigration of Bavarian colonist. It is for this reason that during the first centuries of her existence, the city was referred to as "Bavarian Graz" to distinguish it from "Slavonian Gratz" which is situated in the present-day Jugoslavia. In the second half of the XIIth century, the settlement already housed a market and, some time later, she was raised to the standing of city.

From her very beginning, the city with its fortress, which looms up on the Schlossberg, proved to be an indispensable bulwark toward the Orient. As soon as the XIIth century, the city became the provincial capital of Styria by order of Otkar III, Margrave of the House of Traungaus.

The Otkars - as the Traungaus also called themselves, from the name of the four representatives of the family - met with a sad end. Count Otkar IV, who in 1180 became the first Duke of Styria, died of leprosy at an early age. Having had no children, he named the Babenberg family as the heirs to his lands. And so it was that in 1192, Leopold V of Austria, of the House of Babenberg, assumed the governing of Styria. He too, chose Graz as residence of his princedom.

Leopold V did not have a long while to taste his possession of Styria: in Graz celebrating the Christmas of 1194, while out riding, his horse slipped on icy ground crushing him under its weight. Medical science was unable to save him and he died on December 31 of that same year.

As with many other centres, the urban development of Graz, too, was determined by the Ancient Roman road, which in the Middle Ages still played an important role in the traffic of trade. The road, however, did not cross, as we might suppose, that which in the time following will become the city, but instead passed near the right bank of the Mur, along the slopes of the hilly region called Plabutsch. This, then, was the first important commercial road of the city.

Afterwards, when trade with the Orient became progressively more active, a new road, which from the west pointed eastward, acquired importance. The road crossed the city, passed over the Mur, continued through the present-day Murgasse, and then climbed toward the mountain in the Sporgasse.

And what about crossing the river? It could be said that where there are no bridges, there is no traffic. Such was absolutely not the case, however, because initially, in the spot where in later years the Hauptbruke will stand, there was a ford which allowed the crossing of the river.

It is not known when the first bridge over the Mur was built. Mention of it is first made in 1361. Before this time, however, the river had already been regulated as had its lateral branches, so that areas situated at a lower altitude and consequently up to this time swamps, such as the present-day Hauptplatz and Sackstrasse, had then become liveable.

Around 1240-50, Graz had its first medieval walls. These walls will fully serve their purpose for three hundred years, until, in a sad state of disrepair, they are replaced by more advanced fortifications. These new citywalls are raised by the best military architect of the times, the Italian, Domenico dell'Allio.

Just what Graz with her first walls looked like can be seen in the oldest pictorial view of the city: the painting representing the Scourges - now unfortunately in very bad condition - located on the external southern side of the Cathedral of Graz of 1485.

At this time, the town had really very little space to grow into; only mean farmhouses were allotted to them for this purpose. The Monastery of Rein (the present-day Abbey of Rein near Graz) received the first three of them as a gift in 1164. From these three farmhouses, the Rainerhof, n. 20 of Sackstrasse, was born, the oldest house in Graz.

Very few of the city's foreign friends - as well as many

of the city's own inhabitants - know that at one time Graz was the residence of sovereigns.

The first was Leopold III of Hapsburg who, in 1379, following the first division of the Hapsburg estates, raised Graz to the standing of residence of his governement. Following this, however, something even more important happened: Emperor Frederick III commanded the Holy Roman Empire (of German nationality) from Graz for ten years, and he had the construction of the Burg and the Cathedral begun in 1438.

Frederick III is one of the most unique characters of the Hapsburgs. Of no other member of this family have so many contradictory judgements been formulated by historians. Some define him as intelligent and a believer in miracles, others as persevering and extravagant. It may also be read that he was fearless but not very resolute.

Frederick had little power and even less money, and perhaps it is for this reason that he was so parsimonious. Indeed, he was never able to dispose of large sums of money. He was not even able to undertake his trip to Rome with a suitable following on the occasion of his coronation as emperor. Being the thrifty person he was, he combined his trip to Rome with his proposal of marriage to Eleonor of Portugal who had been brought to him there, and so got married in Italy.

His tendency toward mysticism is probably the reason he had the letters AEIOU applied everywhere, even in the Burg and the Cathedral of Graz. As he never revealed the meaning of these five letters, the most divergent explanations have been given them in the course of centuries. The most noted of them is the one which interprets them as the initials of the expression, "Austria est imperare orbi universo" ("To Austria awaits the right to goven the entire world").

Some decades later, magnificence reaches Graz: with the second division of the Hapsburg estates, Emperor Ferdinand I leaves his son, Charles II, Lower Austria, composed of Styria, Carinthia, Carniole and Istria. From 1564, Graz returns to being a residential city, much more splendid than it had ever been under the parsimonious Frederick III.

Archduke Charles II of Lower Austria is a true Renaissance prince and the years of his reign are among the most significant of Styrian history.

Charles was a great patron of the art of the gunsmithy, a passionate lover of music and especially of hunting. The country estate and hunting lodge of Karlau (today a part of Karlau Penitentiary) was built on his order on the other side of the Mur; he furthermore ordered the building of the Burg. He promoted the breeding of Spanish horses, brought by his father to Lipizza near Trieste, and had Lippizaner horses brought to Graz. Today these horses are bred at Piber in Western Styria.

But all the splendour of the court can not hide the serious state of political problems. Religious struggles break out and the dangerous threat looms up in the Orient: the Turks.

Charles II, Catholic prince, was forced to make concessions to the Protestants because of contributions in money which he needed for defense against the Turks.

Charles' son, Ferdinand, the future Emperor Ferdinand II, however, energetically combatted the wave of Protestantism. He could bring about the Counter-Reformation to the fullest because he did not feel himself bound to his father's promises.

Once the Turkish danger had been averted for good, thanks to two decisive victories (in 1664 at St. Gotthard and in 1683 at the gates of Vienna) the economy began to flourish again, and the splendour of the Baroque Period to unfold. Aristocrats and bourgeoisie alike competed in their aspirations to culture and to the obtaining of posts.

In 1784, Emperor Joseph II issued an edict whereby Graz became an open city. This meant that the walls and the bastion of the city could be torn down.

In the following century, the XIXth, the beneficient action of a Hapsburg in Styria must be mentioned. The effects of the actions of Archduke Johann are felt even today. Even though these deeds are less known than his romantic love story with the daughter of the station master, Anna Plochl (whom he was finally able to marry after long years), the deeds that this popular prince committed as a private citizen are innumerable.

Besides all else, he founded the Joanneum Museum of Graz and purchased the Brandhof near Mariazell. In his creating this farm, he resolved to demonstrate to the farmers how farmland should be correctly run. He then founded the Agrarian Association, the Historical Association of Styria, a professorial chair in mineral and metallurgical sciences. In the years following the Mineral-Metallurgical Upper School of Leoben was born, as well as, and especially, the forerunner of the Technical University (Erzherzog-Johann-Universität) of Graz. Finally, he commissioned famous artists and great personalities to portray and sing the praises of the countryside and of the life of the people of Styria. He made Styrian dress popular everywhere, wearing it himself (the popularity of this costume continues even today).

Even though Archduke Johann has been dead for more than one hundred years (he died in 1859) Styria has not forgotten him. He is remembered not only by the monument in the Hauptplatz.

Industrialization and the connecting of Styria to the railway in 1844 - Styria owes this too, to Archduke Johann - gave a new boost to the economy and brought prosperity to the city. New roads and districts were born and the number of inhabitants climbed rapidly. During the reign of Emperor Joseph II, Graz was still a quiet little town of some 30.000 inhabitants; at the end of the XIXth century there were already 138.000 inhabitants, and today, there are almost 250.000.

In 1938, with the rise to power of the National Socialist Party, a serious regression took place. Graz lost its economic and cultural importance as the "gateway to the southeast". 1938 is also the year in which the provincial capital of Styria was transformed into Greater Graz because of her incorporation of the satellite towns. The "glorious" period, however, ended quickly. Bombings seriously damaged the city: 15% of inhabited constructions were either destroyed or seriously damaged.

In the decades which followed the end of the war, the city got back on its feet, and a fairly good well-being flourished within its walls. New relations were made with the Southeast and the Balkan Countries. New and numerous factories and companies were born. Modern buildings were constructed everywhere and new institutes were opened in the upper schools. In some districts, for this reason, the city completely changed appearance.

Fortunately, however, Graz has remained a garden city, whose greenery invites inhabitants and visitors alike to relaxation and recreation.

THE SCHLOSSBERG

The Schlossberg is without a doubt the heart of Graz: it along with the adjoining Stadtpark forms an island of green in the confusion of city houses. Measuring 473 meters in height, it dominates the Hauptplatz by 123 meters. We may reach its peak by taking the steep path dug out of the rock, starting out from those gently winding paths that begin in the Karmeliterplatz. If this should prove too tiring, the peak may also be reached by way of the Schlossberg's own funicular railway.

Originally, the Schlossberg was a rugged dolomitic cliff without a hint of vegetation. With its stronghold, very little of which remains today, it served to defend the city. The fortress on the Schlossberg was never taken by storm, not even in the summer of 1809, when it was besieged for many weeks by preponderant French forces.

In the same year, however, in accordance with the clauses of the Treaty of Vienna, it was demolished. Only its two towers were saved from destruction.

In the years, 1839-1842, on the initiative of the then divisional commander of Graz, the lieutenant general Franz Ludwig von Welden, the barren hill cluttered with rubble was transformed into a natural park. Thousands of trees and hedges were planted; innumerable paths and roads were made. The Schlossberg had become unrecog-

The Schlossberg: on the right, the Franziskanerkirche.

nizable. Welden, in ill health, withdrew from public life to his beloved Graz in 1851 and there he died two years later. A monument erected in 1859 on the west side of the hill, recalls this man who was so important in the fate of the city.

It is peculiar to note how the fortress on the hill is called "Schloss" (palace) while the residence of the sovereign at the foot of the hill is called "Burg" (fortress). The name Schlossberg appears for the first time in the XVIth century; the residential palace built in the city by Emperor Frederick III was called "Burg", and so it was that the "Burg" on the hill came to be known as "Schloss".

THE CLOCK TOWER

The Uhrturm, being the distinctive construction it is, dominates the Schlossberg. Perhaps you have already run into it down in the city among the souvenirs, as symbol of the city of Graz. The mighty tower is rather old: it was built in 1560.

The Uhrturm houses one of the oldest bells in the country. First called "bell of the condemned to death", it later became "the bell of the loafers". The first name derives from the fact that it rang before every execution. The name "bell of the loafers" was born in the last century because its ringing adverted inns and caffès that it was time to close in accordance with a police order.

If you observe the clock carefully, you will note that the arms on the clockface are reversed: the big one indicates the hours, the little one the minutes. This was done intentionally so that the time could be read from the city below more accurately.

In the past, the so-called "cry of the organ" resounded from the Uhrturm. Around about 1640, in fact, an organ called the "Styrian horn" was placed there which was heard every day in the morning and in the evening , as well as for great festivities. The organ, however, could only produce a single chord, the already-mentioned "cry of organ". Unfortunately, it was lost in 1809 during the French period.

Still in the XIXth century, on the wooden parapet that surrounds the tower, could be found the guard-post for the sighting of fires. When a fire broke out in the city, the guardian would sound the alarm (the bell). The location of the fire was indicated by displaying lanterns, hoisting up baskets or red flags.

If you look down from Uhrturm toward the west, past the low wall, you will see the statue of a dog in stone placed on a pilaster of the terrace of the house below.

His story follows: in 1479, Emperor Frederick III, fearing war, sent his fifteen-year-old daughter, Cunegonde, from Vienna to Graz so that she might be safe in the fortress of the Schlossberg. The King of Hungary, Matthias Corvinus, to

View of the city from the Schlossberg.

The Uhrturm, symbol of Graz. ▶

whom Cunegonde was promised, decided to have her abducted. The captain of the castle, however, who just happened to be completing his inspection round, thanks to the barking of a dog, uncovered the abduction scheme and was successful in thwarting it. A monument was erected to this dog who had been so watchful.

"LIESL" AND "HACKHERLÖWE"

The Glockenturm houses the most famous bell of Graz, the "Liesl" ("Lisette"). The tower was built by order of Archduke Charles II of Lower Austria.

A commemorative plaque placed on the Glokensturm recalls that this tower along with the Uhrturm was saved from destruction thanks to an indemnification of 2,978 florins and 11 kreuzers paid to the French occupational troups by the middle-class tradesmen of Graz.

On the esplanade stands the lion Hackher (Hackherlöwe), a monument which remembers the valiant defense of the Schlossberg against preponderant French forces in 1809 under the command of Major Franz Hackher. The old lion was melted down during the Second World War; the one we see today was placed in its present location in 1966.

the Glockenturm with the "Liesl".

The Bastion of the Cannons.

The Hackher Lion.

8

"STALLBASTEI"

The Bastion of the Cannons (or "Stallbastei"), twenty meters in height, is also an integral part of the Schlossberg. In the distant past, the fortification on the Schlossberg was already utilized as a prison. The Bastion served this purpose as well.

During the years of the Counter-Reformation, the dungeons were filled with preachers, evangelical faithful and their simpathizers. Up until the era of Empress Maria Theresa, political or military prisoners or nobles who had stained themselves with some crime were kept in the Schlossberg. Persons convicted of adultery, duelling, murder, blasphemy, lese majesty and often of high treason, served out their sentences here.

In the second half of the XVIIIth century, the so-called "casemates", utilized in most recent times as an outdoor theatre (they were really the vault of the two-floor cellar beneath the house of the castle commandant), were used as a prison for dangerous criminals.

The "Türkenbrunnen" (Fountain of the Turks) should really be called the Fountain of the Germans, because it was not the Turks who built this 94-meter well from 1554 to 1558, but German miners. At most, some Turkish prisoners of war worked on the well as labourers.

If from the Türkenbrunnen we continue for a bit in a northerly direction, we reach the so-called Starckehäuschen (Little Starcke House). It was so named by a German actor who used it as a summer residence in the last years of the XVIIIth century.

The little house was originally built in 1572 as a powder-magazine. A lawyer of Graz purchased it in 1818 and, from the powder-magazine, he fashioned a house which approaches the Gothic style, for use during the season of the grapeharvest. However strange it may seem, in the last century the grape-vine was cultivated on the Schlossberg.

This solicitor was a very enterprising person. In front of the southerly wall of the Bastion he had a powerful tower built, fitted with merlons and embrasures. He had a sun dial and a fresco placed on the wall of the Bastion, neither of which exists today.

The Bastion of the Cannons: in the foreground, the Fountain of the Turks.

THE HAUPTPLATZ

Today, we can hardly imagine that at one time the area of the Hauptplatz was the flood zone of the Mur, and yet, in the Xth century, this was precisely the situation. By the middle of the XIIIth century, the Hauptplatz was already completely surrounded by houses. Most of these displayed wooden porticoes - which, in later times, were made in brickwork - beneath which merchants put their merchandise on display. Originally the Hauptplatz stretched further than it does today, reacheng as far as the Landhausgasse. The Rathaus had not yet been built.

Besides a lovely wrought-iron fountain next to the present-day Rathaus, toward the middle of the XIVth century, you could also find the pillory, the fool's lock-up and a wooden donkey. To be put in the pillory, to ride the donkey and to be closed up in the fool's iron cage formed the infamous punishment par excellence. Hardened thieves were branded; those found guilty of the most serious crimes were decapitated on the Hauptplatz.

Let's have a look at the Rathaus. Here follows its story: the first Rathaus was built in the Hauptplatz about 1550, after the "Chancellery" located in the ex-ghetto of the present-day Frauengasse. It was a handsome building done in the Renaissance style.

Gradually, the first Rathaus revealed itself too little for a city which was constantly growing. By means of transformations an enlargements, the second Rathaus came into existence in 1806, a harmonious building in the neoclassical style.

The third Rathaus (the present-day one) was built in 1888-1893 and required a new transformation and a new enlargement of the already-existing structures.

This transformation completely unfolded in the spirit of the Gründerzeit. Before taking up the restoration of the facade in 1966, the citizens of Graz asked themselves if the Rathaus should remain as it was, or if it would be more appropriate to restore it to its neoclassical forms with the simple and noble design of an architect of Graz. Here was a unique opportunity to bring a new building to life which harmonized with the old houses surrounding the Hauptplatz.

The majority of the citizens, however, decided to keep the facade which by that time was known and familiar to them.

View of the Rathaus from the Schlossberg.

The Hauptplatz with the monument to ▶ Archduke Johann.

Rathaus. ▶

Glimpse from the Rathaus.

Monument to Archduke Johann.

AROUND THE HAUPTPLATZ

Let's take a little look at the beautiful Hauptplatz which, up to the Rathaus and the house at no. 14, is entirely surrounded by splendid old buildings. In the course of the centuries, its appearance has not changed as is the case for most of the old city. This is probably where its charm lies.

The impressive "Weissche Haus" (Weiss House) at no. 3, situated on the corner to the right of the Rathaus, is also interesting. It was built in 1710 by the banker, Johann Adam Weiss, who went bankrupt in 1729, thus creating a great sensation in the Graz of the time. Parts of the house were handed over to his creditors as living quarters: these were, so to speak, the first condominium apartments in Graz.

The Adler Pharmacy was already built and functioning as the district spice shop in 1535; it is one of the oldest pharmacies of Graz. The "Zur blauen Kugel", ("At the Blue Ball"), located at n. 6, is rich in tradition. It displays a fresco of Saint Christopher painted in the XVIIIth century, and was already mentioned in 1586.

On the northern side of the so-called "Steigeregg" is found, (Sporgasse, no. 1 - Sackstrasse, no. 2), the great and impressive corner building with its old caffè, the "Nordstern." The house at no. 16 in the Hauptplatz catches the eye for its beautiful Baroque facade covered with stuccowork.

The monument to Archduke Johann of course, should absolutely not be forgotten; it has been here since 1878. The design for a similar commerorative monument was elaborated immediately after the Archduke's death in 1859. At first it was decided to place it in the Am Eisernen Tor Square, and in 1870, the first stone was set in place.

It was not immediately decided to raise the monument in the Hauptplatz, in the center of the old city, because here, in accordance with the testamentary dispositions of a baron who died in 1864, a fountain was to be placed there.

Thus a typically Austrian compromise was reached: no, to the fountain alone, no, to the monument alone, yes, to both of them. The inauguration of the monument was a great day, and for the occasion the Emperor himself was present.

The four female figures at the feet of the Styrian prince represent the four rivers: the figure with the sheaf of corn symbolizes the Mur; the maid with the vase, the Enns; the woman with the basket full of grapes, the Drau; and the figure with the cup, the Sann. The two latter rivers are located in what was once Lower Styria.

Here, in brief, follows the story of the house at no. 14: originally, it had a beautiful Baroque facade which, unfortunately, in 1915 was torn down and rebuilt. In the old

THE "LUEGG"

house there lived the daughter of a lawyer, Maria Leopoldina Koschak, who, following an uhappy love affair with the Austrian diplomat, Count Antony Prokesch von Osten, married Carl Pachler, a lawyer from Graz, in 1816. The couple lived in the so-called "house of the crowskinner," today at no. 28 of the Herrengasse. In 1827, the Pachler house hosted Schubert, who dedicated some Lieder to the mistress of the house, herself an expert pianist. Mrs. Pachler introduced a custom to Graz which, up to that time, was unknown, that of decorating the Christmas tree.

The "Luegg" (Hauptplatz, nos 11 and 12) is undoubtedly one of the jewels of the square. The two houses display a rich XVIIth century stuccoed facade. The porticoes date back to he Middle Ages and, like the windows, were originally ogival.

As early as the Middle Ages, the house on the corner was called Luegg, and even Lugeck. In the XVIIth century, it took the name of "Mosseregg" from the name of the owner, Mosser, a rich merchant, and in the XVIIIth century it went back to being called Luegg. Already at that time, the young and the old Graz came together at the Luegg. The theatre playbill was hung here, and millineries and stationery shops could be found in the vicinity. Today, as in the past, the Luegg is a very much frequented meeting-ground.

For many years, not far from the Luegg, in front of the entrance to the Sackstrasse, stood a powerful and twisted Baroque column: the Column of the Trinity. In 1876, because of the increase in traffic, it was transferred to the Karmeliter-

The Landhaus.

The Landhaus: the courtyard. ▶

THE LANDHAUS

platz, where it still stands today.

On the occasion of its inauguration, none other than the famous preacher, Abraham of Santa Clara, delivered his famous sermon. He was active for some time in the monastery of the Augustinians (today of the Domenicans) in the Münzgrabenstrasse.

For centuries, the Hauptplatz has been the scene of a lively market. Buyers and sellers from all countries, even from as far away as Russia, came to the markets of spring and autumn.

The inhabitants of Graz are very proud of their Landhaus, and even visiting foreigners are enthusiastic. It is considered, and rightly so, a Renaissance jewel. The Landhaus, headquarters of the regional government, bears an extraordinary historical-artistic importance for the regional capital of Styria. A great part of the history of Styria, from the era of the Turks right up to the present, unfolded in it. The

courtyard is a masterpiece of architecture and in it, the Renaissance of Northern Italy made its entrance into Graz.

The construction of the Landhaus of Graz unfolded in various stages. In 1494, the Regional States of Styria purchased a building, located on the corner between the Landhausgasse and the Herren-

14

gasse, called the "Chancellery". The relatively late construction of a real Landhaus is due to the fact that in the Middle Ages only mobile Diets were held. They were called mobile in the sense that they had no stabile location, but instead took place here and there, as the case called for.

Very soon the "Chancellery" revealed itself too small, and so it was that in 1519 that part of the construction on the Schmiedgasse was also bought, which is to be considered the oldest part of the Landhaus complex.

The construction of the part containing the Knights Hall (on the Landhausgasse) then followed in 1527-1531, by Italian architects for the first time present in Styria.

The most important section, however, is the construction, after the demolition of the "Chancellery", of the main section on the Herrengasse by an Italian military architect, Domenico dell'Allio from 1557 to 1564. The style of the palace, which shows reminiscences of Venice, reveals that the architect received his professional formation in Northern Italy.

In 1890, in place of a section of demolished courtyard, the narrow and independent communicating corridor with arcades was built which gives a marvelous sense of isolation to the courtyard.

The Landhaus: gargoyle in the courtyard.

The Landhaus: the courtyard with the well.

The Landhaus: windows of the Landstube with the well.

THE LANDSTUBE

Even if you do not take part of one of the sight-seeing tours of the city, organized by the Tourist Board of Graz, the porter at the Landhaus will be glad to show you the Chapel, Diet Hall and the Knights Hall in the Landhaus.

Just one last word about the facade of the Landhaus on the Herrengasse: "Imagine the Herrengasse submerged in water, a few gondolas, the posts in front of the building painted green and white, some reddish drapes hung over the balcony and there you have the view of a Ventian canal". So writes a reporter in 1890.

Without a doubt, a jewel of the courtyard is the well with arcades made of bronze in 1590, and crowned by a knight in arms called "the little man of the Landhaus".

Don't forget the splendid copper gargoyle of the XVIth century which juts out from the roof of the Landhaus.

Not far from the well, in the northeastern corner of the courtyard, is the Landhaus Chapel. This edifice, built in 1630 on the foundations of a previous clock tower can be reached by means of a picturesque stairway.

In the antechamber of the Landstube (part of Knights Hall) you will observe two splendid Spanish heraldic tapestries, once property of the Princes of Eggenberg, and the wall-painting which depicts Em-

The splendid Landstube.

peror Franz Joseph (XVIIIth century) dressed for his coronation.

The most beautiful hall of the Landhaus is undoubtedly the Landstube which, for more than 400 years, has served as the hall for meetings and consultation to the representatives of the Regional Diet of Styria. This hall received its Renaissance appearance in 1530-40. In 1740, the Landstube was transformed on the basis of a plan by an expert Jesuit priest (the high altar in the Cathedral of Graz also bears his name) and so received its marvelous Baroque appearance which it still has today.

Knights Hall (Rittersaal), which for practical purposes was divided in two, is located next to the Landstube. Unfortunately, in the process it lost much of its suggestiveness. At one time, it was used as a hall for special festivities and, in the period 1945-1964 (until the restoration of the play-house), it was also used as a theatre.

The so-called "Noise Tablets", located in the main entrance of the Landhaus, in the Herrengasse, date back to 1588 and prohibit the "unsheathing of the breadknife", scuttles, fighting and din in the Landhaus.

THE LANDESZEUGHAUS

One of the major attractions of Graz is the Landeszeughaus (Regional Arsenal), situated right next to the Landhaus on the Herrengasse. This building hosts one of the richest collections of arms in the world. Already in 1551 in Graz, there was "a refuge for artilleries" as well as many armouries, among which numbered the one in the Landhaus. As time passed, the armoury proved too small, and so the Styrian States planned the construction of a real arsenal which was built in 1644. In the XVIth and XVIIth centuries it assumed great importance when it became the most important armoury of Lower Austria. In 1699, it had to record its maximum

The Zeughaus: the portal.

The Zeughaus: the well
in the courtyard.

The Zeughaus: inside.

Ornamented armouries from
Innsbruck (1550). ▶

Heavy XVIIth century armouries. ▶

The Zeughaus: the complete armour for Count Stubenberg's horse.

capacity at 185,700 pieces of ordinance.

Among the defensive weapons, we find suits of armor, helmets, hauberks and shields. The artisans of Graz alone account for roughly 1,200 of the cuirasses and helmets here. As mentioned earlier, the armor and spur makers lived along the Sporgasse.

In addition, the arsenal houses 2,200 side arms, the deadliest of which are the broadswords, 180 cm. long. Numerous fire-arms and a sizeable selection of valuable portable fire-arms complete the collection.

Today the Arsenal houses about 29,000 inventoried pieces of ordinance.

OLD HOMES OF THE BOURGEOISIE

An attentive eye can still see the many old homes of the bourgeoisie. Characterized by wide pediments, beautiful facades, elegant doors, and pretentiousness, some are even richly decorated it stuccowork.

In the Baroque Period, the well-to-do middle class refused to be suprassed by the aristocracy and so, slowly, the differences between the noble palaces and the rich residences of the middle class began to disappear. The use of stuccowork, previously limited to the inside of buildings, was extended to the outside surfaces under the form of vine-tendrils which completely invaded the facades of buildings, as was the case in the already-

mentioned Luegg.

Many houses were decorated with frescoes. Unfortunately, however, not many have remained, but among those that still do exist the ones in the "Gemalte Haus" ("the Painted House") at no. 6 on the Herrengasse, is well worth a visit. The Saint Christopher on the house at no. 6 in the Hauptplatz, is another decorative attraction.

The "Gemalte Haus" was originally called the Herzoghof, "Ducal Court". This was in accordance with a privilege of Duke Rudolph IV of 1360 to exempt anyone who owned the house from taxes and other duties. The owner of the house, for his part, at his own expense was expected "to raise the throne" to the Lord of the Land whenever the latter resided in Graz. The owner was obliged to take in his Lord and be his host as was befitting of his rank.

At a later date, this feudal concession passed on to the then recently-built Burg, and the tax exemption for the Herzogshof fell out of use.

In 1620, Emperor Ferdinand II assigned the house to his younger brother, Maximilian Ernst to be used as his residence. During this period, the Italian painter, Pietro de Pomis received the commission to decorate the house with frescoes.

Among the various owners that followed in the course of centuries, there was the money-changer, Franz von Lathurner, in the second half on the XVIIIth century, who had the already very damaged frescoes restored. The painter, Johann Mayer of Graz, received one thousand ducats for this difficult task. In our own century, too, the frescoes have been carefully restored twice, in 1929 and in 1949. Fortunately, the two storefronts on the ground floor do not destroy the impression of unity given by the facade.

A characteristic element of the historic centre of the city is the many old inner courtyards which, in recent years, have begun to be cleaned up and reevaluted: indeed a beginning worthy of praise.

From the complete abandon of Baroque exuberance, neoclassicism was born. The careful observer will still find in Graz a whole series of constructions built by the middle class in the neoclassic style. One of the most beautiful is undoubtedly the neoclassic Rathaus (the second) which we have already spoken about.

Allow us just a word about something that confers a particular splendour to the old city: the many Saints and Madonnas which, from the niches of the facades, lead a barely-considered life. They are devotion expressed in stone which rises above everyday profane confusion. These sculptures testify the consolidating of Catholicism after the victory of the Counter-Reformation, in a period in which the Cult of Mary was particularly widespread.

The old city houses not only the idyllic, but its physical representation as well. This can be seen in the noble houses from the period of the Industrial Revolution ("Gründerzeit"). Unfortunately, though, many of the facades of this part of town have been torn down in the course of modernization.

The city, in the meantime, has become aware of its inheritance, and is intent on defending its architectural tradition as well. In this way, her appearance will be able to age intact and dignified.

Gemalte Haus on the Herrengasse.

A romantic internal courtyard in the historic center.

The Stadtpfarrkirche: view of the high altar.

THE STADTPFARR-KIRCHE

If you should happen along the Herrengasse, you must absolutely take a look at the Stadtpfarrkirche. Its full name is Haupt-und Stadtpfarrkirche zum Heiligen Blut (Principle City Parish Church of the Most Precious Blood of Christ). This is a beautiful late-Gothic church with a main hall displaying a nave and three aisles, built at the beginning of the XVIth century as the conventual church of the Domenicans.

It has been a parish church since 1586, the year in which the Domenicans had to abandon it. The Baroque facade of the church dates back to 1742; its interesting bell tower, with a copper roof and two sloping sides, richly decorated with historical scenes, was built in 1781 in substitution of a belfry.

Perhaps not everybody knows that Hitler and Mussolini are portrayed in the Stadtpfarrkirche. When in 1953, the painter from Salzburg, Albert Birkle redid the windows which had been destroyed by bombings, he revealed to no one the identity of the sullen characters which appeared in his great multicoloured windows. The mystery was revealed two years later by a journalist: among the shifty spectators of the scourging of Christ, there are also Hitler and Mussolini

(window on the left side in the area of the high altar, fourth panel from the bottom on the right).

The news appeared in newspaper articles all over the world. Visitors came rushing in throngs to the Stadtpfarrkirche, with and without binoculars.

The main portal is rendered beautiful by a portico with richly stuccoed columns. The impressive statues of the Princes of the Apostles, Peter and Paul, can be seen to the left and right. On the outer wall on the side aisle, we find those of St. John of Nepomucen and Ivo. When the statues of the apostles were hoisted up, an accident took place: the Apostle Paul fell to the ground and broke into a thousand pieces. The sculptor, Joseph Schokotnigg, had to sculpt another.

THE JOHANNESSCHIFF

Entering the church (completely rebuilt in 1875 in the Neo-Gothic style) at the side entrance on the right, we encounter the south aisle, called the Aisle of Johann (Johannesschiff). In this aisle we find an altar-piece which, artistically speaking, is the most valuable of the church. The painting, "The Assumption of Mary," by Tintoretto, was brought to Graz in 1594 thanks to the initiative of his student Pietro de Pomis. Archduke Ferdinand II, son of Archduke Charles II of Lower Austria, donated it to the Stadtpfarrkirche.

It its upper half, the painting shows the Assumption of the Virgin

Am Eisernen Tor Square.

Mary, carried off by angels, while in the lower half, gathered around the empty tomb, the distressed apostles are depicted. The countryside, which appears in the center of painting, provides the setting for an unknown church. This painting, until 1875, was located on the high altar.

The churches and chapels of Graz number about fifty. Many of these may be seen from the Schlossberg. Most of these churches date back to the Baroque Period, few to the Gothic Period. Unfortunately, there are no churches remaining of the Romanesque Period. One of these was the Thomaskapelle (Chapel of Saint Thomas) on the Schlossberg, right next to the Glockenturm, but it was demolished in 1810.

AM EISERNEN TOR SQUARE

The military term "Am Eisernen Tor" (At the Iron Door") indicates that in this place at one time (until 1860), a door by the same name was

found which closed the Herrengasse. This is also recorded by a modern fresco situated on the eastern wall of the headquarters of a firm called Schönbauer.

The powerful door served as a prison. Here, for example, the three actors who in 1773 refused to go on stage because they had not been paid for many months, were imprisoned.

Before the construction of the Renaissance fortifications, the Medieval walls of the city had their doors closer to the center on Graz. At approximately the end of the Herrengasse, in the wall, a little door could be seen, the so-called "Judentürl" (little door of the Jews"). It was so called because the Jewish Ghetto was situated in that area. Beyond the city walls could be found the Jewish cemetery.

Since 1875 there has been a fountain in the square which, one year later on occasion of the seventieth birthday of the poet, Anastasius Grün (who lived in Graz and whose real name was Anton Alexander, Count of Auersperg), was dubbed Auerspergbrunner (Auersperg Foun-

The Landesmuseum Joanneum on the Neutorgasse.

Landesmuseum Joanneum: Chalice of the Alliance.

Landesmuseum Joanneum: Coronet of the Dukes of Styria.

Landesmuseum Joanneum: Carriage of the consort of Emperor Frederick III.

tain). Soon after, the name of the fountain was extended to the square and so it was called Auerspergplatz, but again in 1899 its name was changed again to Bismarckplatz. Today, as we have already said, the square is called Am Eisernen Tor Square.

THE JOANNEUM MUSEUM

If the god of rain plays a nasty trick on you, dedicate a day to the museums. But rain or not, don't go without visiting the Joanneum Museum.

The original center of the Museum is the building at no. 10 Raubergasse. It was built in the

Landesmuseum Joanneum: Peter Brueghel, Holiday in a Dutch Village.

Landesmuseum Joanneum: boiserie and furnishings of a hall of a lordly residence (about 1760).

XVIIth century as the dairy farm of the Saint Lambrecht Monastery and hence its name of Lambrechter Hof. Eleven years later, the monastery sold the building to the field-marshall general, Jakob Reichsgrafen von Leslie.

This sale had very unpleasant consequences. Because the monastery did not have the permission of the Holy See to sell the building, the seller as well as the purchaser were excommunicated. This provision, however, was revoked after a few months.

The Lambrechter Hof has been the headquarters of the Landesmuseum Joanneum since 1811. The museum was founded by Archduke Johann of Hapsburg who put at the museum's disposal his own natura-listic collection which formed the original nucleus. Since the building proved tight for space, anothe was built at the end of the last century at no. 45 of the Neutorgasse.

For many years, the Joanneum Museum grew around the original sections of natural history. The historical-artistic sections and the Alte Galerie (Old Gallery) were located at no. 45 Neutorgasse.

This building too, reached the point of overflowing with objects worthy of being displayed. In 1941, the separation of the collection of objects of the XIXth and XXth centuries from the collection which was at the Landesgalerie, and the transfer of the former to the recently-founded Neue Galerie (New Gallery), located in Herberstein Palace at Sackstrasse, no. 16, permitted the creation of a great section of Medieval Art.

Among the numerous and valuable pieces on display, three deserve special attention.

One of these is the carriage which belonged to Eleonor of Portugal, consort of Emperor Frederick III.

After the imperial marriage and coronation this luxurious carriage, the only preserved Gothic carriage of the so-called "bonnet" form, was to be used by the Empress for her entrance into Graz and into Wiener Neustadt (where another imperial residence was located). Due to the political situation, however, it never arrived there.

Rich in symbolic meanings is the splendid ducal coronet, the oldest of the three ducal coronets found in Austria (the other two are in Innsbruck and in Klosterneuburg). The ducal coronet appears on the sarcophagus of Duke Ernst the Steadfast (father of Emperor Frederick III) in the Abbey of Rein near Graz, and in the painting of Emperor Frederick III of 1441, located in Vorau. The original Gothic lines of the coronet were changed into Baroques forms in 1765 by order of Emperor Joseph II. In 1785, by imperial order, the precious head-dress was taken to the Schatzkammer (Chamber of the

Treasury) in Vienna. Following
insistant requests from the Provincial States of Styria, the coronet was
returned in 1790 and brought back
amidst great festivity to Graz.

We must finally remember the
goblet of the Lanschandenbundes
(National Injury Alliance) which
weighs 12 kilograms, a kind of
tankard made of gold-plated silver.
It was the wedding gift of Archduke
Ferdinand of the Tyrol to his
brother, Charles II of Lower Austria and was preserved as the symbol of the so-called National Injury
Alliance of the Styrian Provincial
States. Since 1895, it has been
housed in the Joanneum Museum.

The altar fragments which come
from the abbey of Novacella near
Bressanone are of considerable
interest for the grace with which
they illustrate scenes from the life of
Thomas à Becket. This photo essay
focuses on the scenes showing the
saint's death and his mortal remains
in the coffin. The altar-pieces may

be the work of the famous South Tyrolian painter and engraver Michael Pacher; one of his most famous works is the high altar of St. Wolfgang in Salzkammergut.

The imposing altar-piece of the altar immediately attracts the visitors eye: it is the great altar of miracles of Mariazell, made between 1518 and 1522 by the Master of the tablet of Martin in Bruck. Until the 18th century, the altar was located in front of the ambo, next to the Chapel of the Graces in the famous Styrian sanctuary of Mariazell. It is composed of 47 miraculous events or facts relating to the Madonna of Mariazell plus a votive image, and is considered without peer in the history of late medieval painting.

The stark simplicity of this large torso of a crucified Christ by the Master of the Crucifix of Mühlau is extremely suggestive. The work dates back to 1320-1325.

Marvelously elegant is the only way to describe the sculpture of the Madonna of Admont (1310), which one art historian defines as "fine, musical, truly Austrian". Perhaps originating in the Upper Rhine region, it is still fascinating today for its aristocratic and refined spirit.

Of great artistic interest are the two Brueghels, "Fair in a Dutch Village" by Pieter Brueghel the Younger, and the "Triumph of Death" by Jan Brueghel.

One example of noble interior

Landesmuseum Joanneum: Crucifix (1320).

Landesmuseum Joanneum: Master of Our Lady of Admont (1300-1310): Virgin with Child.

decorating dating back to 1760 is this so-called Chamber of Maria Theresa, originally from a castle in Mura Szombath (today Murska Sobota in Yugoslavia).

A very interesting section with over 5000 pieces ranging from the gothic to the baroque is dedicated to the art of wrought iron forging in Styria.

29

THE LEGENDARY RAUBER

We have already spoken about the Raubergasse. Thieves (Räuber) did not live here at one time, but rather, the family of the von Raubers. To be exact, they lived in the so-called Rauberhof, the building which today houses the Joanneum Museum at no. 10 Raubergasse. The most well-known personality of the family of the Barons von Rauber was undoubtedly the legendary Andreas Eberhard, of gigantic stature, boyhood friend, confidant, bodyguard and constant companion to the emperor Maximilian II who reigned 1564-1576.

A reporter of the time describes him as follows: "He can rightfully be defined as the German Hercules, because with a generous hand Nature has endowed upon him those rare qualities which the Greeks attributed to their heroes and the Jews to their Samson. Besides his gigantic stature of three cubits, she endowed him with a beard that, when it was divided into two thick braids, it not only reached the floor when he stood but returning upwards it reached his waist".

The physical strength of the legendary hero must have been extraordinary: with his bare hands he broke freshly-hammered horseshoes for sport and, with a single blow of his sword, he was capable of splitting an enemy from his head to his saddle.

The fame of this Styrian hero, finally elected member of the Supreme Council of War, spread throughout all the countries of Europe. Foreigners continually arrived to the imperial court wanting to admire the gigantic baron. The reporters of the day attributed numerous duels to him which the famous hero finished victoriously.

Within little time after the death of the giant, the Rauberhof beame property of the Provincial States of Styria. When the Protestant school, situated in what would later become the Paradeishof, became too small, the States began to build schoolrooms here in the Rauberhof. This school was closed after only four years, at the beginning of the Counter-Reformation.

Landesmuseum Joanneum: wrought-iron transom.

Landesmuseum Joanneum: wrought-iron crucifix.

Landesmuseum Joanneum: valuable iron cassone of 1582.

The Court-house on the Marburger Kai. *The "Houses of Nuremburg" on the Lend Kai.*

IN PRAISE
OF THE CITY

We have spoken about the charm of the old houses of the bourgeoise. There is in Graz, however, a considerable number of buildings which were erected toward the end of the last century, such as the Courthouse or the romantic "houses of Nuremburg" on the other side of the Mur. All of the buildings, though, the old ones as well as those which are "only" one hundred years old, contribute, intact as they are, to creating the charm of this little but great city.

Among cities her equal, Graz flourishes almost in secret. For many foreigners it is just a city to pass through on their way south. And yet, thanks to her marvelous position and her southern charm, she deserves greater attention: usually after a long or brief stay in this serene city, the foreigner is left enchanted.

We meet with extraordinary enthusiasm, though, not only in the present, but also in the past. The Minnesänger (troubador), Ulrich von Lichtenstein is one of the first to celebrate Graz: "To Graz goes my desire," he sings in his "Frauendienst".

The French marshal, Marmont, general in chief of the French occupational forces in Graz in 1805, defines the city as one of the most pleasant capitals of the Austrian States. He furthermore adds: "A well-to-do nobility resides there".

The German poet, Johann Gottfried Seume, who traveled the world over, in 1801 wrote in his famous travel journal, "A Walk Toward Syracuse": "Grätz is one of the most beautiful lands that I have ever seen."

The famous scientist and travelèr, Alexander von Humboldt - to whom a street of Graz is dedicated - defined Graz, with Salzburg, as the most beautiful city of Europe. The younger son of Mozart, Franz Xa-

vier Wolfgang Mozart, composer, pianist and chapel master, lived in Graz in 1820 and wrote in his diary: "The position of Grätz is really most fascinating and it has the advantage of having beautiful...".

The German poet, Friedrich Hebbel, climbed to the top of the Schlossberg in 1847 on the occasion of a visit to Graz and exclaimed: "I doubt I have ever enjoyed a view such as the one seen from the Schlossberg in my entire life".

No less enthusiastic was the Austrian poet, Anton Wildgans who, in 1824, following a trip in the area around Graz, wrote to his wife: "This area is of a unique beauty. I can only compare it with the area around Naples".

A Styrian countess, Purgstall born Lady Cranstoun, in 1834 wrote to her English friends: "Grätz has the most beautiful surroundings of any I have ever known, with the exception of Florence. I consider it, too, the least expensive area of Europe".

31

The Franziskanerkirche.

The Krebsenkellerhof.

THE FRANZISKANER-KIRCHE

The Franziskanerkirche (Church of the Franciscans) is among the oldest churches of Graz. The church and monastery are mentioned already in 1239, and at one time, they were located outside of the Medieval walls.

The great church was completed in 1277, the bell tower with its bulb-shaped cupola in 1643. In 1515, Emperor Maximilian I forced the Minorites to give up their monastery to the Franciscans, who are still there today.

The bell tower houses the oldest bell of Graz, cast in 1272. During the last war, the church was partially destroyed. The modern windows are the work of the painter, Franz Felfer, from Graz.

In 1965, some old houses, which on one side faced the Mur and on the other the Franziskanerkirche, were sacrificed to the new superelevated road.

In one of the demolished houses, no. 10 Neutorgasse, where today a public garden is found, Maria Anna Schicklgruber, the grandmother of Adolf Hitler, worked as maid and cook in the home of the Jewish butcher and soap-maker, Leopold Frankenreiter.

In 1837, she had a natural child, Alois Schicklgruber, who was legitimized in 1877 by the man who in the meantime had become her husband, Johann Georg Hiedler (later Hitler). The illigitimate son of the cook (the father of Adolf Hitler) must have been born of a relation with the son of the cook's employer. This, however, is not historically proven. It is a fact, though, that the young Frankenreiter for twenty years (for fourteen years according to other sources) paid the cook alimony for the boy.

One of the most beautiful and idyllic courtyards of Graz is the one of the house located at no. 12 Sackstrasse, the "Krebsenkeller" ("crayfish cellar"). On warm summer evenings, it is splendid to have a seat and to eat and drink at the foot of the Schlossberg. Already in 1538,

the so-called "Trinkstuben" (drinking halls) existed. A plaque in the courtyard remembers the constructor, Imperial Counsellor, Jörg von Klaindienst of Wachsenneg, who must be considered as the first innkeeper of Graz.

More than one hundred sketches all told, by the painter Robert Foit, together with others by the painter Franz Thür, are found in the publichouse and in the "Foitstüberl" ("little tavern of Foit"). The sketches depict numerous personalities and typical characters of Graz.

You will be surprised by the great number of beautiful portals there are. You may see them in palaces which were once of the nobility and in the houses of the well-to-do middle class, and they attest to a love for decorative and sumptuous particulars no longer felt today.

The portal of Khuenburg Palace (Civic Museum), (top left); the portal of Herberstein Palace (top right); the portal of Attems Palace (bottom left); the portal of the Old Mint (bottom right).

PALACES OF THE NOBILITY

Graz has much to offer her foreign visitors: not only beautiful old houses of the middle class, which we have already spoken of, but many splendid and marvelously articulated Renaissance and Baroque palaces as well.

Graz, as opposed to other cities, did not experience a sudden climb, nor an equally sudden decline. Life within her walls went on tranquilly, even though there were, of course, periods of maximum splendour. It was only under the reign of Maximilian I (son of Frederick III) that the nobles went to live in the city. For the first time, the wide facades of feudal palaces found their way between the narrow and old houses of the bourgeoisie.

During this era, the Italian Renaissance made its entrance into Graz. In a short time, an Italian colony of artists, architects and artisans settled there, and gave their own characteristic imprint to both the inside and outside of a great number of churches and palaces.

The denominational conflicts and the Turkish danger in the XVIth and XVIIth centuries paralyzed all activity in construction.

The construction of buildings was only revived toward the end of the XVIIth century with the blossoming of the Baroque Period.

Attems Palace: the outside.

Attems Palace: the staircase.

The Schlossbergplatz seen from the Schlossberg.

THE SPORGASSE

One of the oldest streets of Graz is the Sporgasse. Since the time it has become a pedestrian zone, it has even further increased in beauty. Now in the open-air, in the midst of old middle-class homes, you can have yourself a tranquil cup of coffee, converse or perhaps reflect on the fact that a few steps up the road, where the Sporgasse branches off into the Hofgasse, is all that separates you from the site of the oldest settlement of Graz.

The name of the Sporgasse is derived from the German word for spur-maker (sporenmachern). This street was especially dedicated to arms: in the XIVth and XVth centuries the makers of arms, armour and bows lived and worked here.

In the centuries which followed, the Sporgasse became the meeting-point for lovers of drink. Here could be found not only two of the then twenty-two ale-houses of the city, but numerous and comfortable hotels.

Observe the Pharmacy of the Stag at no. 10, already in existence in 1564, and the splendid Baroque relief on the doorway of house no. 13, not to mention the copper gargoyle with the dragon-shaped head. No tourist should miss visiting the famous arcaded courtyard, Gothic in part, of the palace of the Teutonic Order at no. 22.

Pedestrian zone of the Sporgasse.

Jugendstil facade on the Sporgasse.

Courtyard of the Palace of the Teutonic Order.

THE TURK
BELOW THE ROOF

Let's stay a bit longer in the Sporgasse. If once we have gotten to the fork Sporgasse-Hofgasse, we follow the Hofgasse and after a few steps we turn around, we will discover the Stiegenkirche (Church of the Stairway) which is not visible from the Sporgasse, because it is so well-hidden. The steps that lead to the church appear as a curious oblique staircase which cuts the facade of the house at no. 12 in half.

Let's walk along the Sporgasse again. The statue of a Turk, from the garret of the remarkable Saurau Palace, looks downward on the unsuspecting passers-by.

There is a legend dealing with the Turks, known by all the children of Graz: during the Turkish siege of 1532, the general, Ibrahim Pasha, was seated on a carpet wining and dining with his following in the courtyard of Saurau Palace. A cannonball, fired from the Schlossberg, landed right in the Turk's plate. The pasha flew into a rage and exclaimed: "If I cannot have this scorching stove (the fortress), I shall never have the cold room (the city) either!". He raised the siege and hurriedly withdrew with his troops.

As we have said, this is only a legend, as Graz was never besieged by the Turks. The figure of the Turk is indeed only a family stigma which exempted the owner of the house from having to quarter functionaries of court.

The "Zur goldenen Pastete" ("The Golden Bun") is undoubtedly one of the most charming buildings of the historic center. Located at no. 28, it houses a much-frequented restaurant. This three-storey Renaissance building at one time belonged to the Protestant barrel-seller, Ruep Dietrich who, in 1590, headed a revolt of the citizens of Graz.

They rose up against a provision of the Catholic, Archduke Charles II which forbade the attendance of their children at the Protestant school.

Saurau Palace: the portal.

Saurau Palace: the Turk.

View of the Stiegenkirche.

A charming Renaissance building, "The Golden Bun".

THE DREIFALTIGKEITS-SÄULE

Not far from the Saurau Palace, you will find the Karmeliterplatz (Square of the Carmelites) which only in 1623, with the moving of the city walls, became part of the city. Already in 1578, Archduke Charles II of Lower Austria decided to found a "new city" here. He called, during the period of the Counter-Reformation, a great number of priests and nuns to Graz. The Monastery of the Capuchins in Paulustorgasse (the street which from the Karmeliterplatz going north leads to the Paulustor), so came to be. Today, this building houses the Volkskundemuseum. The Carmelites went to the "square toward Purkh" and gave their name to it. In 1633, the priests were able to consacrate the church; the convent was added later. What was once the church is still recognizable from the high pediment. A part of the Provincial Archives are found there today.

For one hundred years, until 1796, the Karmeliterplatz was adorned with a commemorative column (which was not, however, the column of the Trinity) in remembrance of the victory of Count Montecuccoli over the Turks near Mogersdorf in 1664. This Column of the Turks, or of Mary (as it is also called), was

The Uhrturm seen from the Karmeliterplatz.

Detail of the Column of the Trinity in the Karmeliterplatz.

Wildenstein Palace, Police Headquarters.

afterwards moved to the Jacominiplatz, and presently has found a resting-place of great effect in Am Eisernen Tor Square.

For eighty years, the square was without decoration, until another column was brought there. The Column of the Trinity (or Dreifaltigkeitssäule) had initially been raised in the Hauptplatz in 1685 right in front of the entrance to the Sackstrasse in sign of thanks for the end of an epidemic of the Black Death. It created a traffic problem there, though, and so in 1876 it was definitively transferred to the Karmeliterplatz.

THE VOLKSKUNDEMUSEUM

At times the Volkskundemuseum (or Museum of Folk-Art) is a bit neglected by foreign visitors, while it should be visited at all costs. There, you may become acquainted with agricultural implements, folk-art (such as ceramics, carving, crèche and farmhouse furniture), farmhouses, religious folk-art (votive offerings, paintings under glass).

The Styria Museum of Folk-Art was founded in the summer of 1913 by Viktor von Geramb who, shortly thereafter, became the recipient of the first professorship of folk-art in German-speaking countries. He can be considered the founder of research into Styrian Folklore.

The Museum stands on historic ground. The headquarters of the Volkskundemuseum was once the old Capuchin Monastery. Even before this, however, there were no buildings, but rather, an open space where in 1600 - during the Counter-Reformation - ten thousand Lutheran books were burned. The mostpart of the 28,000 objects inventoried today are on display in the twenty-six halls of the museum. Among these objects even complete rooms of farmhouses may be seen.

One of the most interesting objects on display is the Heilige Kümmernus (St. Affliction). This Saint is not only found in Styria (as for example is the Geisthal in Western Styria), but also in other churches of Central Europe. St. Affliction is an enigmatic statue, because a saint by this name never existed, nor was such a saint ever canonized by the Church.

Scholars associate her with the Holy Visage found in the Cathedral of St. Martin in Lucca. The Holy Visage, a Medieval crucifix, represents Christ not as the half-naked Ecce Homo, but as a crucified king with a long robe reaching down to his ankles. In later times, the legend was born of the martyred Christian princess who was to marry a pagan prince under order of her pagan father. Imprisoned, she prayed God to give her a beard to spoil her own beauty. So it was that during the night, she indeed grew a beard which excited the loathing of her bethrothed. Her father, exasperated, ordered her crucified.

Therefore, the entire story is only an erroneous interpretation of the Holy Visage of Lucca.

Steirisches Volkskunde Museum:
"Saint Affliction".

Steirisches Volkskunde Museum: old
Styrian costumes.

THE STADTPARK

Many are the roads which lead to beneath the mighty Paulustor (Door of St. Paul). This is the only door of the Renaissance fortification still in existence; it was built in 1623 by Emperor Ferdinand II.

Graz is envied, and rightly so, by many cities for the Stadtpark, this magnificent natural park in the English fashion of considerable size. It is more than one hundred years old and was created on the area of the once neutral ground, in recent times used as a drill-ground, which lay in front of the glacises. The idea for the park was born in the last century, and belongs to the burgomaster of Graz, Moritz Ritter von Franck.

The crowning part of this public park, rich in tress, shrubs and flowers is undoubtedly the Stadtpark-brunnen (Fountain of the Stadt-park), which the city councellors acquired in 1873 at the World's Fair held in Vienna. The side-parts of the fountain, cast in Paris, can still be found today in the Place de la Concorde in the French capital.

In the vicinity of the fountain, you will find a simple one-storey building. At one time it was a very frequented caffé, but in 1960 it was to be torn down. A group of young artists was successful in saving it and, giving it the name of "Forum Stadtpark", they created a center for avantgarde cultural events. The association "Forum Stadtpark" since 1961 has published a literary periodical, "Manuskripte", considered to be one of the best avant-

garde periodicals in the German language area.

There are numerous monuments of famous personalities of the past and the present. The present period is represented by the busts of the composer and orchestra director, Robert Stolz, born in Graz, and of the poet Franz Nabl, well-known beyond the borders of Styria, who died in Graz. The two allegorical figures near trhe fountain of the Stadtpark, "Austria" and "Styria" were originally located (until 1970) on the old Hauptbrücke, the oldest bridge of the city.

Outside of the Paulustor.

The Stadtpark: the fountain.

The Stadtpark: "Styria" and "Austria".

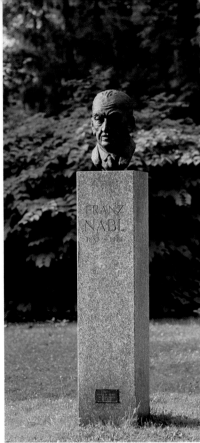

Especially during the cold season, the animals in the Statpark allow people to walk right up to them. Numerous squirrels, which in Graz are called "Hansi", but also blackbirds, chaffinches and titmice come up to the visitors to fearlessly take food from their hands.

The Stadtpark: bust of the composer of Graz, Robert Stolz.

The Stadtpark: bust of the Styrian poet, Franz Nabl.

View of the "Forum Stadtpark".

The Opera-House.

THE OPERA-HOUSE

The Opera-House is very interesting both inside and outside. It is still relatively young, having been built in 1899 by two Viennese theatrical architects who created it in the style of Fischer von Erlach.

In 1944, it suffered a bombing, and the reconstruction lasted from 1945 to 1948. However, the entrance-hall with columns crowned by a tympanum had to be sacrificed.

The inside, with boxes and gallery, is characterized by a charming white-red-gold triad in a sumptuous Rococo decoration. In the past of the Opera-House of Graz, many world-famous artists have been acclaimed, and for many of them, it has served as a springboard to an international career.

THE FREIHEITSPLATZ

The best way to reach this square, if you come from the center of town, is first to take the Sporgasse and then the Hofgasse. In so doing, you will walk right into the Freiheitsplatz (Liberty Square).

An unusual and beautiful wooden portal, crowned by a two-headed eagle, will certainly catch your eye in the Hofgasse. This is the once court bakery of Edegger Tax which has existed since 1569 and, therefore, is the oldest bakery of Graz.

Liberty Square is one of the most beautiful squares of Graz, tranquil, secluded and harmonious. In the past, it was completely built over. To the east, in the place of today's Theatre, there was once the Theatre of the States which was completely destroyed by fire on Christmas night in 1823.

The Provincial States of Styria not only immediately rebuild the theatre, but they also created this beautiful square.

The square was finished around 1840. At the time of completion, it was called Franzensplatz, from the name of the Austrian emperor, Franz I.

On the northern side of the square, in 1838, an impressive building was built which at one time belonged to the Abbey of St. Lambrecht and which, for this reason, today is called Lambrechter Hof.

The figures in the tympanum of the neoclassical building have a symbolic meaning. The builder, Georg Hauberrisser the Elder, had many rivals in his profession, but an influential patron as well, the head of the architect guild, Lindner, Lindner promised Hauberrisser to help him obtain the official title of architect. This friend is depicted in relief in the robes of the angel that indicates the eye of God. The young boy is the master builder, Hauberrisser. The first four dogs are the rivals and enemies of the architect. The last little dog, sitting tranquilly

The oldest bakery of Graz.

The Freiheitsplatz with the statue of Emperor Franz I.

The Cathedral.

to one side, represents the only architect who was not contrary to Hauberrisser.

Among the amusements of court in Graz, there was once the game of "pallacorda", a kind of tennis played indoors which the emperor, Ferdinand I brought to Vienna from his native country of Spain. In that period, in Vienna as well as in Graz, many buildings for this sport were erected. One of these can be found on today's Ballhausgasse which leads into the Freiheitsplatz.

THE CATHEDRAL

The Cathedral is the most valuable of all the churches of Graz. Already in 1174, in the spot now occupied by the Cathedral, there was a Romanesque construction, the old St. Gilgenkirche, which at the time was still situated outside the city walls. The church was consacrated to St. Aegidius (commonly referred to as St. Gilg), patron saint of tradesmen. In times past, public legal hearings were held both inside

and in front of the church.

Emperor Frederick III, in place of the Romanesque building, had the present structure erected in the years between 1438 and 1462. This is a late Gothic hall-church with tiered roof. The architect was the Swabian, Hans Niesenberger. Up until 1830, the Cathedral was completely surrounded by a cemetery wall.

The Cathedral, up until the XIXth century, had two communicating corridors: one from the

45

church to a wing (which no longer exists) of the Burg which stood in front of it, and one to the west which lead to the presbytery passing above the Bürger-gasse.

In order to embellish the outside of the church, which was rather unadorned, frescoes were painted on the walls. The western facade, where the main entrance in the Gothic style is located, was richly decorated with frescoes which are still visible in the Scourges of God, located on the southern side, the only one of these frescoes still in existence which even though hidden behind a niche, has been ruined by inclement weather. We refer to the fresco painted in 1481 by Thomas da Villach which presents the oldest view of city of Graz. The fresco records the fears of the year 1480: the invasion of the locusts, the horrors of war (the Turks) and the Black Death. It represents one of the best creations of the great late-Medieval painting in the Alps. While under restoration in 1871, the painting was ruined by a layer of wax: the colours were suffocated. Another attempt at restoration in 1913 also failed. Fortunately, a good reproduction in reduced scale of the Fresco of the Scourges exists in the Mausoleum.

The three scourges, however, did not come all together in 1480: records left by historians simplify things a bit on this point.

The locust, in truth, arrived in 1477. In swarms as thick as clouds they completely devastated the fields, meadows and trees.

For two hundred years, Styria was manaced by the Turks, and more than once they invaded the country killing, sacking, putting to sword and burning. The year 1480 was for Graz a "year of the Turks". The enemy arrived right in front of the provincial capital of Styria, but absolutely did not think of attacking. As the walls were "well-armed", they continued on their way.

The Cathedral: the old fresco of the Scourges.

The Cathedral: reproduction of the fresco of the Scourges.

The Cathedral: main portal.

The Black Death, too, which Graz feared but by which she was never devastated, came under the Scourges of God in 1480. Still today, many commemorative columns recall it.

THE HIGH ALTAR

Originally, a Gothic altar was found here which was later replaced by one of the Renaissance style. This latter altar, a mighty construction in carved wood, was donated by the duchess, Maria of Bavaria, consort of Archduke Charles II of Lower Austria. The church originally was the church of court as well as that of the Order of the Jesuits who were called to Graz by Archduke Charles II in the period of the Counter-Reformation.

The Jesuits removed the Gothic furnishings (twelve altars); they also removed the Gothic partition wall and built Renaissance altars which later were to give way to today's Baroque altars.

In the center of the high altar, we find a painting depicting the patron of the church, St. Aegidius. Included among the poor, depicted in the painting, we can note, to the lower left, even a mother nursing.

After the suppression of the Jesuit Order, the church was raised to the level of Cathedral in 1786, after the episcopal seat had been transferred from Seckau to Graz.

THE ORGAN

Looking at the organ, situated on the western women's gallery, it is difficult to imagine that behind the Rococo decoration there is a modern piece of work. It was placed here in 1978. The "regal instrument", furnished with 70 registers and 5,158 pipes, a carillon and a clavicymbal was built by an artisan of Bonn.

Among other things, the Cathedral has never had a bell tower distinct from it, but only a belfry built in 1653. The original cemetery, surrounding the church, reached out a ways into the Hofgasse. After taking over the church from the Jesuits, when the parishioners had to transfer to the Church of the Most Precious Blood in the Herrengasse, the holyground became superfluous and the walls surrounding the Cathedral were moved closer to the church.

The Cathedral: high altar.

The Cathedral: the nave and the organ.

THE NUPTIAL CASSONES

If you should visit the Cathedral, we advise you to absolutely not neglect the most important work of art in the church, the two reliquaries of the XVth century. We refer to the nuptial cassones of Paola Gonzaga of Mantua who, in 1477 at the age of seventeen, became the wife of Leonardo di Gorizia.

The couple chose the Bruck castle at Linz in the Western Tyrol as their residence, where the husband, however, rarely lived and where Paola died when she was barely thirty years old. Leonardo di Gorizia, who with his wife's money paid his own debts, donated the nuptial cassones to the Order of the Knights of St. George at Millstatt in Carinthia. From there, they were transferred to Graz by the Jesuits.

Pope Paul V, in 1617, donated some relics to the Hapsburgs in sign of thanks for having brought Styria back to Catholicism. And so it was that the two cassones, chosen as suitable containers for the relics, became reliquaries and were placed in the Cathedral.

The cassones, in oak wood, present precious ivory engraving and inlaid bone, and are one of the most important works of Italian carving

The Cathedral: choir-stall.

The Cathedral: one of the two valuable reliquaries.

The Cathedral: the Vision of St. Ignatius, by Pietro de Pomis.

of the XVth century. The figures are inspired by a poem by Petrarch, "Triumphi", chosen by Paola Gonzaga who possessed a good knowledge of Latin. The Triumph of Love is an opus of the young Andrea Mantegna; the other works are after his school.

In 1873, the reliquaries were sent to the World's Fair held in Vienna where they aroused such enthusiasm that it almost took a fight to get them back to Graz again.

The Mausoleum.

THE MAUSOLEUM

In the opinion of the author of these lines, here Graz is very Italian: we can see it as we climb the stairs which lead to the Mausoleum and as we view the Baroque facade and the cupolas covered with a green patina. A southern atmosphere dominates around this splendid building. Indeed, we are faced with the work of an Italian.

Archduke Ferdinand, son of Archduke Charles II of Lower Austria, and future Emperor Ferdinand II, commissioned it. The building of the Mausoleum was begun in 1614 on his order on the site where the graveyard-chapel consacrated to St. Catherine was situated. The building of it was frought with trouble.

The Italian court painter and architect, Pietro de Pomis, was commissioned to build it, but died before the completion of the opus in 1633. A master builder continued the construction and raised the slender bell tower. This master builder, Pietro Valnegro, died in 1639, two years after the emperor, Ferdinand II had already been laid in the crypt.

For decades, the construction stood incompleted and suffered considerable damage because the windows had been improperly

49

closed. Only in 1687 did the emperor, Leopold I commission the famous Austrian Baroque architect, Johann Bernhard Fischer von Erlach to complete the arrangements on the inside.

The consacration of the Mausoleum and its altars only took place in 1714.

Let's first have a look at the outside of the building. The Baroque facade on the west with its impressive size is the center of attention. A bigger than life statue of St. Catherine with two angels on either side with laurel crowns appears on the arched pidiment.

The building is composed of two parts: the Katharinenkapelle (Chapel of St. Catherine) and the Gruftkapelle (Funerary Chapel). The first is in the form of a Latin cross and has a barrel vault. Angels engaged in the Eternal Adoration of the name of Christ are depicted in a fresco on the vault of the ceiling. The marvelous stuccos and the high altar are the work of Fischer von Erlach.

Let's turn to the aisle. The subjects of the frescoes which decorate it are the liberation from the Turks (Vienna 1683) and illustrations of the undertakings of the emperor, Leopold I.

The funerary chapel with its elliptic plan (a rather unusual plan for the time in which it was built) now houses the tombs of the bishops. The rich stucco decoration as well is probably the work of Fischer von Erlach. Scenes of the Resurrection of Christ can be seen on the cupola.

A painting which depicts the Wise Virgin and Mary, done in 1847 by the Styrian artist Josef Ernst Tunner, exponent of the Matarene school of painting, hangs on the wall to the left of the entrance.

Tunner, who at the time of his commission was at the height of his career, had made a vow on the occazion of his favorite daughter's (Sylvia) scarlet fever to dedicate a painting to the Cathedral if the child were saved. His prayer was answered.

The Imperial Crypt can be reached by taking a staircase down. In the center of the crypt is placed the marble sarcophagus, built by an Italian artist, with the statues of Archduke Charles II of Lower Austria and his wife Maria of Bavaria, parents of the emperor, Ferdinand II. In truth, Maria of Bavaria alone is buried here; Charles II rests in the Abbey of Seckau.

Only in 1782 was the sarcophagus brought here from the then convent of the Poor Clares (today Pradeishof), when the convent was suppressed by Joseph II.

The Mausoleum: high altar by Fischer von Erlach.

The Mausoleum: cupola of the Chapel of St. Catherine.

The Mausoleum: Imperial Crypt. ▶

THE BURG

Once, the Burg was much bigger than it is today. Not much remains of the old and once vast complex of buildings today.

The Burg was built in 1438-1452 by Frederick III who resided many years in Graz. At first a "palatium" (residential building) was erected near the church (today's Cathedral). Then a construction, situated higher, in the form of a castle was built, and in later years was called the "Friedrichsburg". It was located in today's Freiheitsplatz, at no. 4, on the spot occupied by the Lambrechterhof today.

Emperor Maximilian I, son of the emperor, Frederick III, enlarged the Burg in 1494-1500. For one hundred years, until 1600, construction was continued until there was a vast complex of buildings.

Only the Karlstrakt (wing of Charles, from Charles II of Lower Austria) and the Burgtor (door of the Burg) remain of this complex today. In 1853-54, many buildings were demolished, among them the gala staircase built in 1554 by Domenico dell'Allio (architect of the Landhaus).

The Burg lived a period of splendour as the residence of Archduke Charles II, who came to the throne in 1564. It remained the residence of the sovereigns of Lower Austria until the court was moved to Vienna in 1619.

In the first courtyard of the Burg, on the wall to the right of the Wing of Charles, we find on a scotting a tombstone with a poetical epitaph written in Hebrew script:

"Sadly sings my cithara and its voice is hushed in sadness for the entrance of the president of the court and wise master, Rabbi Nissim, son of Rabbi Aaron, into the eternal resting-place on the twenty-seventh day of the month of June in the year 147 since the Little Number, in the six thousandth year. May his soul be wrapped with the cords of life. Amen". According to our calculations, this happened June 27, 1387.

After the second time they were chased from Graz, in 1496, the Jews were allowed to return to the city only toward the middle of the XIXth century.

Absolutely do not neglect to visit the tower of the north wing (passage-way in the second courtyard of the Burg), where the famous Gothic double winding staircase, built in 1500, is found.

THE LEECHKIRCHE

The Leechkirche is located a few minutes on foot from the Stadtpark and is almost hidden. It was preceded by the Chapel of St. Cunegonde, already extant in 1202. Shortly thereafter, in 1233, the Teutonic Order was founded in Graz. The Babenbergs sought to win the Order to the cause of the defense of Austrian borders against the Hungarians. Duke Frederick II of the Babenberg offered the Chapel of St. Cunegonde at Leech to the Order. Of the Orders which bore the mark of the cross, the Teutonic Order was the most powerful, even though the other two, St. John of Jerusalem and the Knights Templar, were the oldest.

The Chapel of St. Cunegonde was probably destroyed in 1250 during a Hungarian invasion. It is certain, however, that construction of the Leechkirche began in 1275. Only in 1500 were the two bell towers added.

The Leechkirche is considered the oldest church in Graz and a jewel of Gothic architecture. The Madonna with Child (about 1290) with Romanesque reminiscences, found in the tympanum of the portal, and the splendid windows of the XIVth century are of particular interest.

The Burg with the main entrance and the Burgtor.

The Burg: the famous double winding staircase (1500).

The old Leechkirche.

The Leechkirche: Our Lady on the portal tympanum.

The Leechkirche: large windows with glass of the XIII-XIVth Century

The Neo-Gothic Herz-Jesu-Kirche.

The Mariahilferkirche.

THE HERZ-JESU-KIRCHE

Looking south from atop the Schlossberg, over the sea of houses of Graz, the church which most catches the attention is the Herz-Jesu-Kirche (Church of the Sacred Heart) with its high Gothic bell tower.

For a long time a decidedly negative evaluation had been placed on the "historisist" style, with its recourse to esthetic elements of preceding periods, such as in the Rathaus and the Herz-Jesu-Kirche. Today, on the other hand, we view this period of art with a certain indulgence, letting it "live" as a testimony to history.

The Herz-Jesu-Kirche, a Neo-Gothic construction in red brick, unusual for our parts, was finished in 1891. The project was by Georg Hauberrisser the Younger who, as architect and royal professor in Munich, had built among other things the Rathaus of that city. His father, Georg Hauberrisser the Elder, was an appreciated builder in Graz. For the mostpart, the sculpures which decorate the church are the work of Hans Brandstetter, at the time, the most famous sculptor of Graz. The bishop who commisioned the construction, Johannes Swerger, is buried in the crypt.

MARIAHILFER-KIRCHE

For centuries, Mariahilf, after Mariazell, was the most frequented sanctuary of Styria where emperors and popes came to pray. In 1515, the friars of St. Francis of Assisi, called Friar Minors or Minorites, had to leave today's Franziskankirche in Graz in favor of the regular churchgoers. A nobleman, Seyfried von Eggenberg, donated his summer resisence to the Minorites in difficulty, then located in front of the city, where today the church and Monastery of Mariahilf are found.

Already in 1515 there was a chapel dedicated to Mary. Archduke Ferdinand (future Emperor Ferdinand II) with Prince Ulrich von Eggenberg had today's Mariahilferkirche (Church of Our Lady of Help) built in 1607-1611 under the direction of the architect Pietro de Pomis. In 1744, in place of the original Renaissance facade created by de Pomis, modelled after San Giorgio in Venice, the present-day magnificent Baroque facade with two towers was built.

The Baroque high altar with the miraculous image, this too an opus of Pietro de Pomis, is particularly interesting.

THE MINORITEN-KLOSTER

The Cloister of the Minorites, attached to the Mariahilferkirche, presents two real artistic tidbits. The first is the Baroque Schatzkammerkapelle (Chapel of the Treasury).

A copy of the miraculous statue of the Mariahilferkirche is found on the altar, and on the ceiling a view of Graz in which the "Mother of the City" is suspended in the sky. Numerous other frescoes depict miracles done by Our Lady of Mercy.

The second jewel is the Summer Refectory located in the back wing of the cloister, the so-called Hall of the Minorites, with its great staircase of honor, which is one of the most beautiful halls in Graz. It is older than the Chapel of the Treasury and was built in 1691. The author here, too, was Italian.

Besides the splendid frescoes on the ceiling, we see scenes of the Old Testament on the windows all associated with the subject of food. On the frontal wall a gigantic oil paint-

The Hall of the Minorites (once refectory of the Mariahilf Convent).

The Chapel of the Treasury.

Old ostensorium of the Diocesan Museum.

ing stands out, "The Miracle of the Multiplication of Bread".

The Hall of the Minorites is often used for cultural events. A "Maria-hilf Cultural Center", conducted by churchmen, organizes religious and cultural initiatives in the city. A Diocesan Museum is also housed in the cloister.

THE UNIVERSITY

In the days of monarchy, Graz was the city where high functionaries and officials withdrew into retirement: for this reason, it was jokingly called "Pensionopolis". Today, Graz is no longer a city of pensioners, nor has it been for quite some time, but rather of students. At present, about 20,000 persons study at the University of Graz; of this number 1,000 are foreigners. Some 5,200 persons are enrolled in the Technical University, and of these, 600 are foreigners.

Shortly, the University of Graz will celebrate its four-hundredth anniversary from the founding. The first university was an upper school of a religious order. Archduke Charles II of Lower Austria called the Jesuits to Graz and in 1585, he founded the Jesuit University as an instrument of the Counter-Reformation.

Under Emperor Joseph II, the Jesuit University was dissolved and declassed to the level of a "lyceum" (secondary school). Only in 1827, under the emperor, Franz I, was the lyceum again raised to the status of university.

So the name "Karl-Franzens-Universität" was born in remembrance of the persons who founded and renewed it.

As the building in the old university had for some time proven insufficient, a grandiose solution to the problem was decided in the Seventies of the last century: a new university quarter was created. The main building was inaugurated by emperor Franz-Joseph in 1895.

These buildings however, which at the time of their construction seemed so large, as time passed proved to be too small and scanty.

New Institute of Anatomy of the University.

Main building of the University.

Just think that the university had been built some hundred years prior (many institutes already existed before the construction of the main building) for one thousand students, and today it must accomodate a number twenty times as much.

Since the Seventies, many new and modern institutes have been built, such as the Institute of Anatomy. The University of Graz has a great reputation to defend. In point of fact, five Nobel Prize winners have come from its files: Fritz Pregl, Otto Loewi, Viktor Franz Hess, Erwin Schrödinger and Karl von Frisch.

MODERN BUILDINGS

For centuries, Graz consisted only in what today is the historic center of the city, which was at one time enclosed by walls. The suburbs grew very much outside of the city, separated as they were by a wide neutral military ground. Only some time after Graz had been proclaimed an open city by Emperor Joseph II in the XIXth Century, were the walls, bastions and almost all of the doors torn down.

The districts on the outskirts began to grow toward the inside of the city, with the exception of Jacomini, which developed to the south of the fortification moat. In the last century, the first considerable transformation of the city's physionomy took place, because the districts surrounding the historic center were joined to the city. At that time, Graz had six districts.

Looking down at the city from atop the Schlossberg you can grasp how much the city has grown. Inhabited modern buildings and residential centers are born in all districts of the periphery. So it is, too, that the sky-scraper of the post Office in the Mur district ruins an old and welcoming residential settlement. Were they outside of the center, on the outskirts, the eye would better tolerate them.

St. Peter, residential center of Graz.

Hall of the Ursuline Convent.

Church of Thondorf.

The Kalvarienkirche.

The group of the Crucifixion on the Kalvarienberg.

There exist, however, positive examples of modern buildings and correct positioning of them, as is the case with the terraced residential center located at Graz-St. Peter, or the one with an atrium at St. Veit which blend harmoniously with the surrounding environment.

The modern Catholic Pedagogical Academy, or the bold hall which serves many purposes in the courtyard of the Convent of the Ursulines at Eggenberg, are exemplary, in perfect harmony with the palce in which they are located.

Many new churches, too, are the work of expert architects.

THE KALVARIENBERG

North of Graz, at Gösting, on the right bank of the Mur, is found the picturesque and tiring to reach Calvary which for centuries has called numerous believers, especially during Lent. Generally speaking, it is little known even to the lovers of Graz, and foreigners visit it very rarely.

A legend is associated with its creation: the devil once went to Africa to get a gigantic boulder with which he intended to make the Schöckel, the mountain of Graz, higher. When, as he flew over the territory of Graz, he saw a procession below, full of wrath he threw the boulder to earth which broke into three pieces. One of these formed the Schlossberg, one the Reinerkogel (destination of splendid walks from Graz) and the last formed the Kalvarienberg.

At one time, the mountain was called Austein and was the property of Baron Ferdinand of Maschwander. In 1606, the Baron permitted a cross to be placed on the peak. So many faithful streamed to the place that in time a church and the stations of the Way of the Cross were also built.

A reporter wrote in 1816: "Even forty years ago, it was not rare during Lent to see fanatics of all social groups, half-naked, walk the Via Crucis. They bore heavy wooden crosses and with whips lacerated their backs."

The scene of the Ecce Homo on the balustrade of the church, of a vigorous Baroque style, and the group of the Crucifixion on the top is particularly interesting. The statue of Christ, an opus in relief in gold-plated copper of 1775, until 1827, was located on the Hauptbrücke.

The Holy Staircase is found in a portico near the church, and is open only during Lent; the faithful may climb it only on their knees.

The inside of the beautiful Baroque church, behind the high altar, presents a scene of the Mount of Olives from the middle of the XVIIth century, and in part the actual rock of the mountain.

On the high altar in the Dismaskapelle or Mariatrosterkapelle (Chapel of Our Lady of Solace) can be found a statue of Our Lady, probably a copy of the miraculous statue at Mariatrost, which we shall speak of later.

THE STRASSGANG

The fortified Church of Strassgang lies to the south of the city. The church, situated on a hill, rises on old historic ground: at one time there was a "castellun" there, and at the foot of the hill passed a Roman road.

The Church of Strassgang is the oldest on the territory of Graz. If you have heard that the Leechkirche is the oldest church of Graz, do not be confused. This is indeed true considering the situation of the city before 1938, before, that is, Graz incorporated the near-lying areas. Since that date, however, the oldest church of Graz must be considered the Strassgang.

The Church of Strassgang was already documented in 1074. The square fence at the base of the bell tower (built in 1743 in Baroque style) and the beautiful Romanesque nave date back to this period. The miraculous image located in the church has been a destination of pilgrimages for centuries.

Around about 1460, the church was enlarged and redone in Gothic form. The inside was embellished with an interlaced ribbing vault and the Gothic area of the high altar was added.

The parish-house, a building in the shape of a castle, is late-Gothic and has a beautiful portal. Well-preserved Romanesque stones are still visible on the external walls of the church.

Our Lady of the Protective Cloak on the high altar is of particular interest. Among the characters which appear in this group of sculture, finished in 1519, on the left is seen Pope Pious II and, on the right, Emperor Maximilian I with his characteristic hooked nose.

The most well-preserved, if not the most beautiful, Gothic tombstone of old Graz, belonging to Jörg Gradner (1476), can be seen to the left of the high altar. The Gradner Knights decorated the church in sign of gratitude for a victory over the Turks.

Parrish-church of Strassgang.

The miraculous, Our Lady of the Protective Cloak.

MARIATROST

Mariatrost (Our lady of Solace), occupying its marvelous spot, is truly a mandatory visit for the lovers of Graz. It is one of the most frequented sanctuaries of Styria and it is also the preferred church for the celebration of many wedding ceremonies.

From the beginning, flocks of pilgrims rushed in from all the hereditary Austrian dominions, especially from Hungary and Croatia. Still today, the sanctuary is famous even beyond the borders of Styria.

The miraculous statue on the high altar was made about 1465, probably in Italy. When, during the reign of Emperor Joseph II, it had to be restored, the monks had a copy made by a sculptor of Graz. This copy, in a manner which is still unclear, became the property of a member of the middle-class and today is situated in the Chapel of Mariatrost on the Kalvarienberg.

In the last century, heated discussion arose around the question as to which church possessed the original, and which the copy. Today, no one speaks of it anymore.

The Sanctuary of Mariatrost.

Main portal of the church.

The miraculous statue of Our Lady of Solace.

ST. MARTIN

On a low spur of the Buchkogel, west of Graz, snuggled in a charming setting, is the Castle and the Church of St. Martin. The church presents an artistic curiousity but we shall speak of this later.

The castle was mentioned for the first time in the XIth century. In the procession of time, it belonged both to nobles and the Church. Since 1144, it has belonged finally to the Abbey of Admont.

In the XVIth century, the Castle underwent numerous transformations; in the XVIIth century it was demolished for the mostpart and rebuilt in its present-day aspect, which is that of the early Italian Baroque. Instead of building a chapel inside the castle, a church was built next to it.

Numerous noble personages have been hosted in the Castle of St. Martin in the course of the centuries: the emperors Leopold I and Franz I, as well as many Archdukes.

The castle was purchased by the Land of Styria in 1936, after the churchman, Joseph Steinberger, in 1914, had already founded there the first public educational center of Styria. The building, which suffered serious damage during the last war and was rebuilt in 1950-52, today is the headquarters of the Public Educational Center of the Land of Styria.

Let's now turn to the church. The temple was built in 1642 in Renaissance style with a pointed roof of Gothic inspiration.

The artistic curiosity we mentioned above is a tripartite altar surmounted by a horse, work of the great Styrian sculptor, Joseph Thaddäus Stammel, on the occasion of the complete restoration which took place in 1738-1740.

In the center, the altar shows St. Martin, a young Roman soldier, on horseback as he divides his cloak with a poor man. The Fall and the Conversion of St. Paul is seen on the podium on the left side, while on the right, St. Aeligius, bishop of Noyon, patron saint of blacksmiths, attaches the leg of a horse.

Church and Castle of St. Martin.

Altar of the Horse in the church.

THE SCHLOSS EGGENBERG

You must absolutely not miss visiting the Schloss Eggenberg, on the western outskirts of Graz, because we are surely dealing with the largest and most beautiful castle of Styria.

It already existed in the XVth century and was larger; it was then skillfully transformed to its proto-Baroque form as confirms a recent finding of a series of Medieval parts of the building.

The Schloss Eggenberg was built in 1625 by Hans Ulrich von Eggenberg on the basis of his own plans and those of Pietro de Pomis.

Hans Ulrich came from a well-known family of tradesmen whose members were all famous and successful men. An ancestor of Hans Ulrich, Balthasar Eggenberg, was director of the mint under Emperor Frederick III; Ruprecht von Eggenberg was one of the greatest condottiere of the XVIth century; Seyfried von Eggenberg was burgomaster of Graz.

The career of Hans Ulrich, however, was the best. As a close confidant of Emperor Ferdinand II, in 1625, he obtained the post of Governor of Lower Austria. Two years prior, he had been raised to the rank of prince which drove him to build a home where he could receive official visits, the Schloss Eggenberg.

Hans Ulrich von Eggenberg took pleasure in numerical games: the castle presents 4 angular towers (representing the four winds), 365 windows (the number of days in the year), 24 conference halls on the second floor (representing the 24 hours of the day) with 52 windows (the 52 weeks or Sundays of the year).

The castle, since 1939, has been the property of the Land of Styria, and in 1947, it was incorporated into the Landesmuseum Joanneum. It underwent restoration in 1947-1953 because of damage during the last war and the occupation. The Hunting Museum is situated on the first floor, and it is well-known even beyond the borders of the country.

The Schloss Eggenberg.

The Schloss Eggenberg: courtyard.

THE RECEPTION HALLS

The reception halls situated on the top floor of the Schloss Eggenberg are a true delight for the eye (they may be visited only with a guided tour).

The reception halls present some 600 ceiling frescoes all told. The great banquet hall, where the oil paintings by the court painter of the Eggenberg, Hans Adam Wëissenkircher (XVIIth century), are framed in stuccowork,is particularly magnificent. The paintings celebrate the importance of this princely line with two allegorical cycles, placed around a central painting which depicts Apollo on the Chariot of the Sun.

About eighty years after Wëissenkircher, the original painter, Johann Baptist Anton Raunacher of Graz frescoed many halls, decorating a theatre, a game-room, a ballroom, a hall with hunting scenes and one with scenes of gallantry set in the park.

In the succession of the rooms are found small Chinese and Japanese drawing-roms, a hall with heraldic mantles embroidered in gold, a sumptuous bedroom where even Maria Theresa spent the night, gold-white Rococo stoves and chairs and sofas of valuable workmanship.

THE RITUAL CART OF STRETTWEG

A protohistoric masterpiece is located in the section of the Schloss Eggenberg dedicated to prehistory and protohistory. This is the Ritual Cart of Strettweg, so called for the area in which it was found (Strettweg, near Judenburg in Styria). The cart was part of the funerary outfitting of a great burial mound in the period of Halstatt and was discovered in 1851 by a farmer.

This valuable piece dates back to 700 BC circa, and could have been added to the tomb toward the end of the VIth century BC.

The Schloss Eggenberg: reception halls.

The Schloss Eggenberg, the Museum: ritual cart of Strettweg.

CONTENTS